THE SMUDGE
MY STORY

told through

Andrew-Glyn Smail

Published by:
Smail & Van Rossem
2 Endeavour Drive
Bellingen NSW 2454
Australia

ISBN: 978-0-646-52850-2

Additional information:
www.thesmudge.net

Dedication

To my best mate, *Dubu*, the little guy. May you and your humans be blessed with joy for many years to come!

IT ALL STARTS...

on a farm in the centre of New Zealand on Waitangi Day. The humans are out on the streets celebrating. I have just been born! Of course, some silly people will claim that the country is celebrating its birth. Clearly, they must be grown-ups. Alternatively, they must have some other problem.

My first human is a doctor. He cuts off my tail before I've even left the litter. This is my introduction to the human approach towards animal health care. It makes a visible impression on me.

Then he throws me out of the house. Clearly, I have also made an impression. Perhaps it is the big one on the Persian carpet in the living room.

At an early age I am given to another human as a gift. Clearly, one human's gift is another human's reject. I am learning a lot about humans.

Naturally, I am a very special gift. My new human has a strange way of showing his appreciation though. He lays me on my back, spreads my legs and exposes my most intimate parts. And I am still only a puppy!

I am allowed to choose my name. My human reads out a long list of really silly names, until he finally gets to mine. I bark and am given the name I choose: Smudge.

Not just any smudge. I am *The Smudge*.

I decide to call my human Pa. He has a partner. I decide to call her Ma. Both interpret their names as *Woof*. Really, humans do have a serious communication problem.

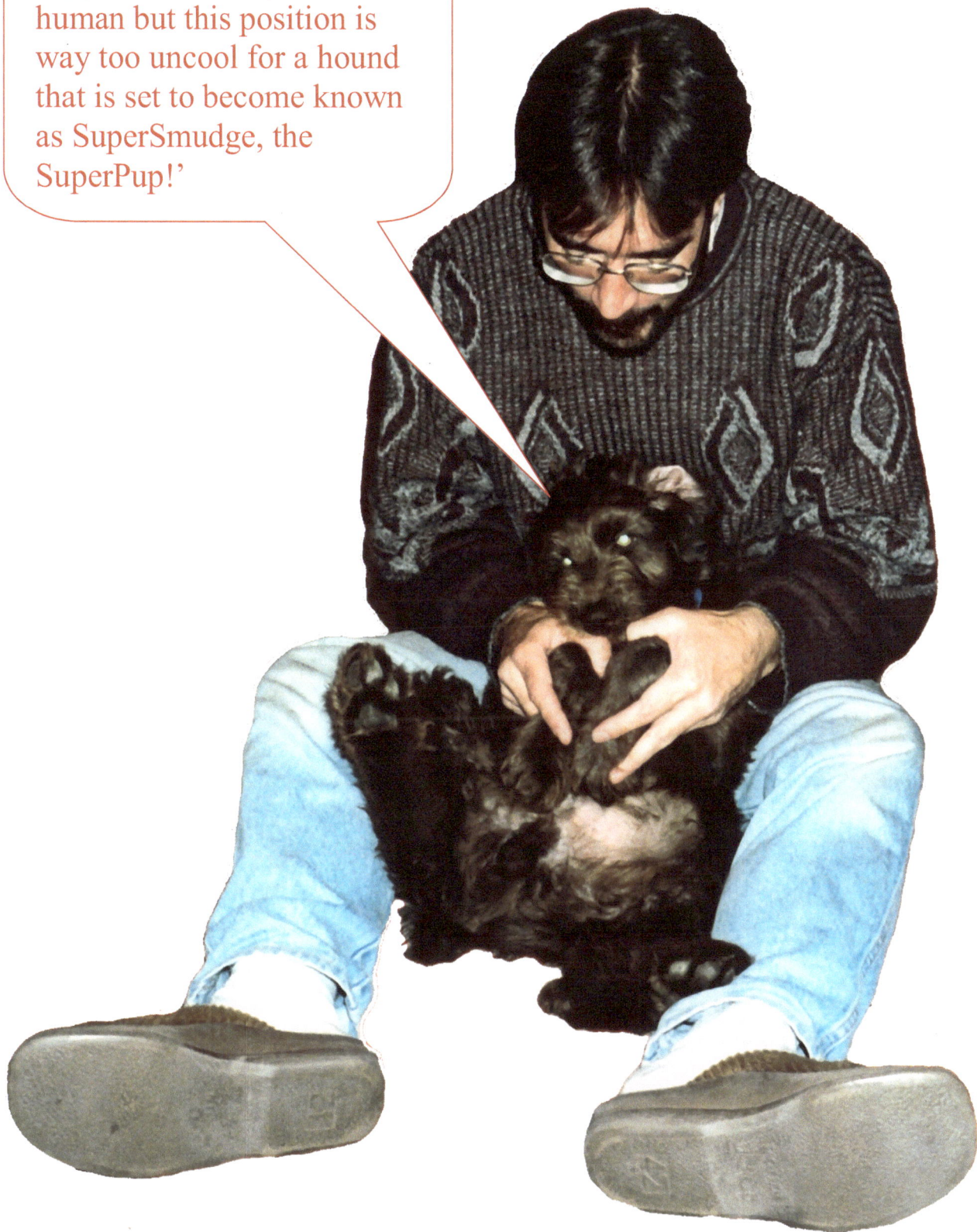

'Look mate, I know you're supposed to be my new human but this position is way too uncool for a hound that is set to become known as SuperSmudge, the SuperPup!'

I AM PRINCE OF THE BEACH...

although you wouldn't say so, given the number of times I am run off my paws by the many dogs that come to take their humans for a walk.

Wherever I go the dogs line up to play with me. The girls fall all over me and the boys simply have to get over it.

It is clear that I have been born to become a star. Yet, it saddens me that so many humans will not have a chance to find pleasure in my presence. After all, there is only one of me.

Life on the beach has its difficulties, as it has anywhere else. The grass lining the dunes presents a thorny problem or rather problems.

Grass seeds! I am attacked by them. Time and time again they worm their way into the thick hair between my toes. There they briefly wait before piercing my skin and digging slowly into my tender flesh.

My suffering is great and it is frequent. It is clear that I have been sent to save the world through my suffering or to do something equally important, such as giving veterinary surgeons the opportunity to improve their surgical skills. And they do.

The vets perform one operation after the other on me to remove the grass seeds from my paws. This has to stop before there is any truth to the rumours that I am an anaesthetics junkie.

Then my humans introduce me to the forest and I am saved. I discover the joy there is to be had with the products of the forest. Trees are used to make paper and...

Go on, admit it: they don't come cuter than this!

I LOVE THE TEXTURE OF PAPER

Not just any paper, mind you. It needs to serve a purpose. Take toilet paper for instance. Humans produce a great deal of what this paper is designed to hold. Then they use some other type of paper to write about it and call it a newspaper. Clearly, a lot of it happens, because the newspapers are always full of it, as are the humans involved.

There always seems to be a long, fresh roll hanging in the loo. Being the smart pup that I am, my education in paper improves by leaps and bounds.

Right through the living room the roll unwinds until I pounce on the final sheet just in front of the bookcase and discover my next adventure in paper. Literature with a capital 'L'. Lots of it. Row upon row of books wait to be devoured. I acquire a taste and appetite for literature!

There are big books, small books, thick books and thin ones. Not for me the slim, lightweight, travel reading matter. No, I prefer something substantial, something meaty, something that you can really sink your teeth into. And I do! The depth of some writing holds great appeal, especially if it is bound in hard cover.

I find one and I rip through it at a tearing pace. All great literature offers something to chew on. This is no exception. Although it is a mouthful – after all, it's Shakespeare's collected works – I am dogged in my determination.

I literally gobble the cover and wolf down the dog-eared pages. Other literature follows until I discover the scrunching texture of the great outdoors in numerous yellow-framed volumes of *National Geographic*. I shred a path through the countries and regions of the world, when suddenly I find myself...

'Ah, toilet training! This will come in handy to keep track of things: a paper trail to keep a record of Smudge fudge production!'

IN THE GREAT OUTDOORS...

My humans banish me to the garden, so ending my literary career.

The time has come to explore the outside world. Perhaps I will discover my true mission in life. I crisscross the lawn sniffing each leaf and blade of grass. Each plant and flower I inspect. Under every shrub and bush I closely examine the earth.

Yet nowhere do I find a sign of my mission. The worms are no help and neither are the beetles. So too the butterflies floating prettily by. 'I am...,' one creature starts. 'We are...,' they chorus. Perhaps the answer lies with a bee.

I SEARCH FOR MY MISSION

I find some bees buzzing amongst the flowers. The air is thick with them. Tirelessly they hover amongst the petals, their wings humming endlessly. I listen. Nothing about a mission here.

Being a bee is all that keeps bees busy. Perhaps the answer is within me, not in a single place but wherever I go. And then it dawns on me. My last good book before being thrown outside was *Hamlet*, a play posing a curious question: 'to be or not to be'.

Not to be is simply out of the question. And if I am to be, to really be, then I may as well be happy!

AND THEN I GROW UP...

but not before I am almost killed. True greatness is born of intense suffering. If The Smudge is really to be, to live life to the full, he first needs to die, or pretty well come close to it, so that he can be reborn.

I almost die before I am a year old, and come close to being reborn. Real life has a way of being really corny at times: it starts to resemble a book.

Some human leaves a box of painkillers on the worktop in the kitchen. The idea seems to be that small pups cannot reach the worktop. Clearly, someone has forgotten to teach the human that small pups grow into big dogs.

To cut a long story short, I almost get to experience – or not to experience, to be more precise – the second part of Hamlet's question: 'not to be'. Pa rushes me to the vet and so begins a dark chapter in my young life.

I am literally as sick as a dog for days on end. I shall spare you the details of how it feels, the sense of swimming in a pit of used cooking oil, the sharp pain. I shall not trouble you with details of my body heaving, of the vile stench of a spreading pool of vomit. I shall not describe the sense of drowning, the utter exhaustion.

Yet I survive. I emerge into the light and am virtually reborn. Both I and my human come to appreciate how it feels 'to be'.

To be is to be happy and to celebrate this I am showered with bones. Not only yummy, they also make a great toothbrush. Check out the teeth.

And so I rejoice in my life, grow up...

'So can we go to the forest now? There are a couple of possums I know who are just dying to meet me and naturally I am willing to oblige....'

AND LEARN TO DANCE...

'Help, not that position again! No, no, you can't. You shouldn't. It's uncool! Aw shucks, just this once then....'

AND GET INTO THE DRIVING SEAT...

literally, as you can see. But why would you want to be in the driving seat? Being in the driving seat allows you to control where you go and how fast. Which means that you can take others for a ride, as it were.

But being in the driving seat looks like a lot of hard work. Not if you are smart. Why not let someone else do all the hard work? Why not get into the driving seat without having to drive?

So how do you get into the driving seat? The first step towards getting into the driving seat is not to want to do so. That's the easy part. Look how uncomfortable it is. You have that big, round thing sticking into your personal space, you can't stretch out, and you can't relax. So I'm not going to drive. Now what?

Now get someone to drive you wherever you want to go. Look at me. I need shelter. My humans give me a home. I need food. They lay on a feast every day. I need health care. They arrange the best. I want to go to the beach. They drive me. I want to go to the forest. They drive me there too. So how do you get them to do that?

How? Easy, become everyone's favourite passenger! Admit it: you love someone who just goes along for the drive. They're relaxed, appreciative, non-threatening, have no hidden agenda and, what's more, you're doing a good deed and you're in control. So how do you become your own favourite passenger?

How? Even easier, be like me! Hop in the front to pose for a cute photo, then jump in the back, where you'll find me ... in the driving seat ... just being me ... just happy old me ... and now you too!

I ALLOW MY HUMANS TO GROOM ME

Glorious coat, isn't it? Now try and imagine how much of the beach and forest I drag home with me. I have this long, fine coat, the kind that some animals literally die for. It retains everything, unless it is groomed for an excruciatingly long time.

My humans insist that, if I want to come inside, the beach and the forest have to remain outside. They say that love always demands sacrifice. This is mine.

Love is being with my humans and grooming is my sacrifice for love. So the beach and the forest remain outside and my humans get to enjoy my presence.

Lucky humans!

AND THEN MY HUMANS REALLY PUT ME TO THE TEST...

They give me lunch, then say I'm not allowed to eat it! Well, it looks like lunch. And he has arrived in a box. A bit on the small side, mind you. And the colour, or rather the lack of it, looks a bit suspect. Still, I'm a broad-bellied fellow: I can tolerate variety.

Perhaps this is one of those fancy dishes they serve in France: small and tasty. Must be. The humans say he's French: bichon frisé. I'm not fussy. I'll take him whatever they choose to call him on their fancy French menu.

So I bend down to get a whiff of the little creature. And as I breathe in, what does he do? He presumes to smell me! I am not used to my lunch savouring me. It is against the natural order of things and, as such, quite intolerable.

What to do? I hesitate and at that moment my humans speak....

Well, actually, I'm quite happy to skip lunch this time. Or any time, rather, if the little guy is lunch. What I mean is, he's not lunch, now or ever. Honest, he's here to stay.

What else do you do if your humans tell you the alternative is life in the doggie box?

So much for being in the driving seat....

'Doggone it! The humans have brought me lunch. Now let's just have a sniff and....'

HE IS A FAST LITTLE FELLOW...

'Huh? Where'd he go? So what if I'm a hunter. Lunch isn't supposed to move, once it has been served!'

'What? I'm not allowed to eat him? I've got to play with that? Hey, this ain't fair. I've got a reputation to keep!'

BUT THEN HE LEARNS TO PLAY...

AND AFTER PLAY IT'S TIME TO REST.

THEN THE HUMANS TAKE US TO A DOG SHOW...

me, the hound of semi-unknown parentage, and the little guy with his tail-long, blue-blood pedigree. There I learn that a dog show is more about humans than it is about dogs.

Washing, clipping, grooming ... humans in their hundreds employ every skill and gimmick to rid their pedigree pooch of everything which looks, smells, or is in any other way reminiscent of dog.

Yet it is I – and not the pedigree pups – who steal the show, that is, if their owners' coos of admiration are anything to go by. Small wonder: by the time they are ready to show their creations...

I am the only dog left at the show! And they dare to call me a mongrel....

'The little guy won "best of breed". Of course, it has nothing to do with the fact that he was the only one of his breed at the show!'

BUT YOU CAN'T KEEP THE DOG OUT OF A DOG...

'It's all the little guy's fault. I was just praying that my daddy would show up with my pedigree papers, so I can also win 'best of breed' at the dog show, when the little guy told me that we had to rush off and chase something furry and because it is my duty to protect him, I had no choice but to go along and....'

FROM SHAGGY SMUDGE ...

That's parents for you. When I am shaggy, they say that I have the blood of sheep in me. Inherited, not ingested although, being the hunter that I am, there are some tongues that wag wickedly.

The first response of a human to seeing me is to gasp in awe, which is of course quite normal.

The second is to request an explanation for such a unique natural phenomenon. 'Immaculate conception', might not be the most accurate reply but it would save me from what usually happens next.

Gazing at my shaggy coat (wavy if I've just been groomed), Ma and Pa ritually reply that I was born in the centre and on the national day of a country which has 16 sheep to every human, that my mother was a Weimeraner but that they have no idea what my father was. Drum roll ... then comes that woolly line:

'We suspect his daddy was a sheep!' the folks chortle. And they spin this tale without feeling sheepish!?!? In the meantime we have moved to a much warmer climate. Now they sheer me. Not just once, mind you but every six weeks for most of the year!

Now that the wool is gone, you'd think they would ease up on the sheep story. No way! They fleece it bare!

Where they would once point to my shaggy coat to stress the sheep connection, now they point to my shorn coat and do the same. Shaggy one day, shorn the next – you can see the sheep in him!

TO SHORN SHEEP

THEN THE BORDERS ARRIVE...

and they actually come as boarders too! They come to board with us until we can find a new home for them.

The border collies are visitors from next door long before they become boarders. Then our neighbour starts dumping them over our fence for days or weeks at a time.

Anyway that turns out to be just the thin edge of the wedge. He is a sailor: frequently at sea in more ways than one,

He then sells his property on condition that the borders are part of the package. Not wanting to jeopardise the deal, our new neighbours take the borders but make plans to dump them with a relative in the city.

Ma goes ballistic: you can't do that to a border collie that's been born, bred and kept on the land. Multiply that by two!

Our humans decide to take the borders until they can find them a new home. I could have told them. No one in their right mind is going to want a creature whose sole purpose and meaning in life is sheep.

No one takes them and so the boarders become residents.

AND STAY AS RESIDENTS

I AM AWARE OF MY AGE, WHEN...

it is not me that brings home the rabbit stew but the little guy. Admittedly, it's a small bunny. It wouldn't even rate as a snack, much less a meal. In fact it's a tiny thing and may not even be a creature at all.

Not that I care to catch any furry creatures nowadays. There are simply too many much more important things to do. My domain encompasses an expanse of lawns, a budding orchard and a fecund rainforest. Growth surges through it all. The grass is thick with heat and moisture, branches bend to their fruit, and the canopy-shaded undergrowth is heavy with promise. Then there are the comings and goings of humans and horses, rabbits and reptiles, birds and bees. All require constant attention.

The little guy is doing remarkably well for a puppy who, like me, was diagnosed with cancer and given only a few months to live as little as five years ago. Still, one must give credit where it is due, I suppose. Clearly, I have been a good influence on him.

Cancer? In both dogs? Drastic action was called for. We went raw! Our humans promptly tossed out the conveyor-belt fast foods! And they brought in fresh meat, fresh vegetables, fresh fruit, grains and massive bones (yep, the genuine article). Yum! Not only is it all delicious but we get to live to enjoy it too ... even years later! And I don't even have to hunt for it!

THE LITTLE GUY UPSTAGES ME

I VAGUELY RECALL...

There is something about the texture of paper that still draws me. Paper, the texture of it ... in the mouth. A lifelong infatuation, you might say, which is of course not quite the same as revisiting one's youth in old age.

Interesting how there always seems to be at least two completely opposite ways of viewing the same issue. Take a roll of toilet paper for instance.

Life is a toilet roll: a seemingly endless supply of blank sheets on which youth can leave its mark. And you do, make your mark that is ... all over the place, each fresh, white sheet inviting you to fill it in your own personal way.

Then towards the end you feel a need to look back, to nuzzle your package of experiences, pry it open and savour them. Yet with each passing day the past fades. Memories slip away and the marks disappear. You know that they were there but increasingly you find yourself munching on blank sheets again. You come full circle.

Only one thing left to do: be in the moment ... savour the paper ... delight in its texture. You can't remember the past? There is no need to. Simply relive it as you see fit.

There is something about the texture of paper that still draws me....

DOING SOMETHING SIMILAR IN MY YOUTH...

I AGE GRACEFULLY...

and put it down to the happiness that others have found in me
and I in them.

I recycle the world's joy in me and spread it where I can. It is a
huge responsibility but I am willing to share it with you. Here, take it,
play with it and pass it round!

THIS IS THE LAST PICTURE EVER....

Within 36 hours I die just after midnight in the middle of the most terrifying storm. It's a scene right out of the movies. Pa carries me from the vet out into the howling night. Rain splatters us both, lightning splits the dark and thunder echoes his bellow of grief. So it goes....

Here you can see me playing

Look closely, all you need is a little imagination....

'Is there life after death? Silly question. You should see the place in the small rainforest where the little guy and my humans last looked on my body in the damp earth. It is bursting with life!'

www.ingramcontent.com/pod-product-compliance
Lightning Source LLC
Chambersburg PA
CBHW041236040426
42445CB00004B/47